A CLICK OF BEETLES

For Isabella

Copyr.ght © 2025 by Stephanie Lipsey-Liu.
All rights reserved
No part of this publication may be reproduced or transmitted in any form or by any means, electronic or mechanical, including photocopying, recording, scanning or otherwise, or through any information browsing, storage or retrieval system, without permission in writing from the publisher.

First printed 2025

ISBN 978-1-917565-06-6
Little Lion Publishing UK
Nottingham, England
www.littlelionpublishing.co.uk

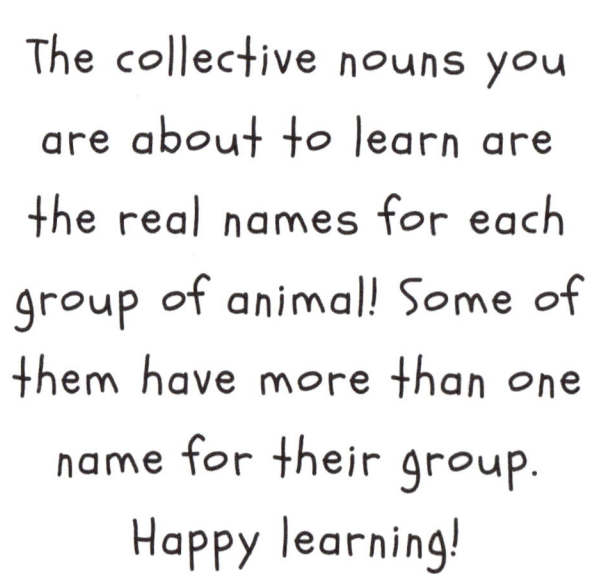

The collective nouns you are about to learn are the real names for each group of animal! Some of them have more than one name for their group. Happy learning!

This Little Lion book belongs to

....

A loveliness of ladybirds

Black, orange, yellow or red;

A loveliness gathers where flowers are spread.

A group of ladybirds is called a "loveliness" or sometimes a "bloom".

Ladybirds are part of the beetle family. There are more than 5,000 kinds of ladybirds around the world.

The bright colours of a ladybird warn predators that it might be poisonous! When frightened, it can release a smelly yellow liquid that tastes horrible. Sometimes, a ladybird will even play dead to escape being eaten.

Ladybirds eat tiny insects called aphids which are often green.

Aphid

In winter, ladybirds hibernate to keep warm and safe.

2

A walk of snails

A foot on the bottom and eyes on stalks;

A group of snails is called a walk!

Snails cannot see very well. They can only see light, dark, and a little bit of movement.

Snails produce mucus, which they leave behind in a slimy trail. This slippery slime helps them glide smoothly along the ground.

Snails are some of the slowest creatures on Earth.

Just like humans need calcium to make their bones strong, snails need calcium too! Calcium helps their shells grow hard and strong as they get bigger.

Snails are nocturnal, which means they sleep during the day and come out at night. They are also very strong. They are able to lift things up to ten times their own weight!

A kaleidoscope of butterflies

Butterflies flying, their colours so bright;

A kaleidoscope dancing in shimmering light!

The smallest butterfly is only 2 cm across.
It is called the "Western Pygmy Blue".
The largest butterfly can grow up to 25 cm across.
It is called the "Queen Alexandra's Birdwing".

Queen Alexandra's Birdwing

Butterflies use the sun to warm up their wings before they fly.

Butterflies taste with their feet! This helps them know if a plant is poisonous. If it is safe, the butterfly can lay its eggs there.

 Can you remember what a group of ladybirds is called?
Turn back to page 1 to see if you were right!

A business of flies

Buzzing, flying and working all day;

A business of flies won't sit still, they say!

Like butterflies, flies can taste with their feet. They can also walk on walls and even ceilings!

Unfortunately, flies can spread diseases to humans because they often land on things that are rotting or dead.

Have you ever wondered why flies are so hard to swat? Their brains can process 250 images every second, while humans can only process about 60!

Houseflies cannot eat solid food. Instead, they squirt out digestive juices to break it down, then slurp up the liquid through their long mouthpart, called a proboscis.

Proboscis

A housefly only lives for about a month.

Flies can see all the way around them. Their eyes are always open because they don't have eyelids.

Can you remember what a group of snails is called? Turn back to page 3 to see if you were right!

A whisper of moths

"Did you hear, Susan was out with Jemima yesterday?!"

Moths are so quiet, their wings barely sound,
A whisper of moths floats softly around.

Moths were around before the dinosaurs! Fossils show that moths have been here for more than 190 million years.

There are about 160,000 different species of moths in the world!

The Luna Moth has no mouth and never eats! After it comes out of its cocoon, it only lives for about a week. This is just long enough to mate and lay eggs.

The largest moth is the Atlas Moth, which can grow up to 30 cm across! The smallest moth, called *Stigmella maya*, is only 1.2 mm across.

Luna Moth

Like butterflies, moths have wings covered in tiny scales.

Can you remember what a group of butterflies is called? Turn back to page 5 to see if you were right!

A click of beetles

A beetle is stuck upside down on the ground,
With a click it flips and is right-side around.

Click beetles can flip themselves the right way up if they get stuck on their backs. This makes a loud clicking sound, which also helps them escape predators.

About a quarter of all animal species on Earth are beetles!

Firefly

Most beetles eat plants. But ladybirds are a type of beetle that eats smaller insects called aphids.

Fireflies are a type of beetle that can glow in the dark. They make their own light and use flashing patterns to signal to other fireflies.

Beetles cannot see very well, so they mostly communicate with sounds or pheromones (special chemicals).

Can you remember what a group of flies is called? Turn back to page 7 to see if you were right!

The UK has over 500 species of non-biting midges and about 150 species of biting midges. Only the females bite!

Bats and swallows love to eat midges.

Midges are common in damp places such as bogs and marshes.

Midges are just 2–3 mm long and live for only about a month. They cannot fly if the wind is stronger than 5.5 mph.

Can you remember what a group of moths is called? Turn back to page 9 to check if you were right!

A wriggle of worms

If you see worms together you can call them a squirm,

A bunch, a bed or a wriggle of worms.

Worms often bunch together to make a layer of mucus that protects their skin from drying out when there is little water. They also huddle to keep warm, and to avoid drowning during floods.

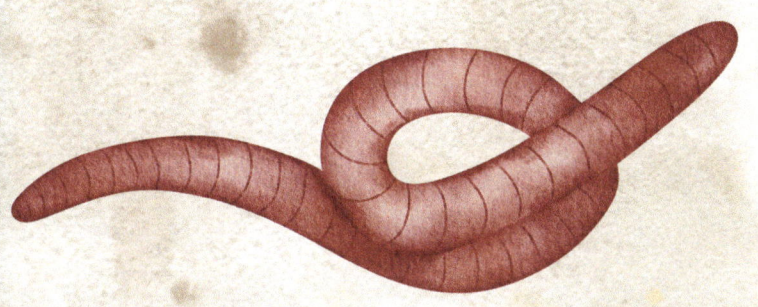

Most common worms have both male and female parts, but they still need another worm to make baby worms.

Worms have existed for 600 million years! Some African worms can grow as long as 6.7 meters.

Worms don't have lungs; they breathe through their skin.

Worms are important for keeping soil healthy. They make channels for water and air, help get rid of dead leaves, and make natural compost for plants.

Can you remember what a group of beetles is called? Turn back to page 11 to check if you were right!

A bed of scorpions

Scorpions are not insects you know;
They are arachnids and some of them glow!

All insects and arachnids have a hard exoskeleton. Did you know that adult scorpions glow under ultraviolet (UV) light! This is because of a thin layer of "hyaline" on their exoskeleton. Baby scorpions have soft exoskeletons that don't glow.

Scorpions can live for about five years and are common in hot, dry deserts.

Scorpions are arachnids and have eight legs. Spiders, ticks, and mites are also arachnids.

To catch food, scorpions grip their prey with their pincers and then sting it with their tail. Scorpions are venomous, and some have venom strong enough to kill a human! They only attack if they feel threatened.

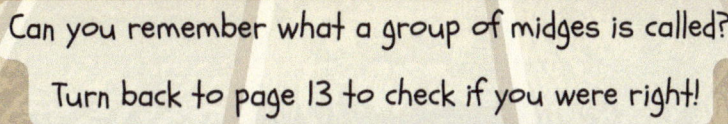

Can you remember what a group of midges is called? Turn back to page 13 to check if you were right!

A clutter of spiders

Spinning their silk with patience and care,

A clutter of spider webs float through the air.

Some spiders are nocturnal (awake at night), while others are diurnal (awake during the day). Some are crepuscular (awake at dawn and dusk), like rabbits.

Jumping Spider

Spiders have exoskeletons, like scorpions. This means both spiders and scorpions must moult as they grow. Their old outer layer comes off, and a new, larger one forms.

The part of a spider that makes its silk is called a "spinneret."

There are about 40,000 different types of spiders in the world.

Spiders can have up to eight eyes. Some have six, some four, some two, and some cave-dwelling spiders have no eyes at all!

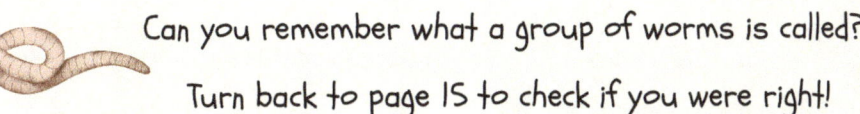
Can you remember what a group of worms is called? Turn back to page 15 to check if you were right!

A swarm of wasps

Wasps carry pollen from daisies and clover;

Helping the garden grow brighter all over.

Most wasps live alone. These are called "solitary" wasps. Other wasps live together in nests. You can also call a group of wasps a "nest of wasps."

Wasps feed on nectar and rotten fruit. Wasp larvae eat small insects, which worker wasps collect and bring to the nest.

Only female wasps can sting.

Wasps rarely swarm together like bees do. But we still call a group of wasps a "swarm."

When we think of wasps, we usually picture yellow and black ones. Some wasps can also have green, blue, or red markings.

Can you remember what a group of scorpions is called? Turn back to page 17 to check if you were right!

A plague of locusts

The locusts land where the wheat stalks sway;

Nibbling the grains as they munch all day.

Locusts are a type of grasshopper that usually live alone. But sometimes, they can swarm in groups of billions, destroying entire fields of crops.

People eat locusts in many countries, and they are a good source of protein.

Locusts are great at jumping because of their strong back legs.

Locusts can eat their entire body weight in food every day. They are herbivores, which means they only eat plants.

Can you remember what a group of spiders is called? Turn back to page 19 to check if you were right!

Glossary

Aphid – A tiny insect that ladybirds eat.

Atlas Moth – The largest moth in the world, with wings up to 30 cm across.

Beetle – An insect with a hard outer shell called an exoskeleton.

Bloom / Loveliness – A group of ladybirds.

Calcium – A mineral that helps humans build strong bones and helps snails grow strong shells.

Crepuscular – Animals that are awake at dawn and dusk.

Exoskeleton – The hard outer covering of insects, spiders, and scorpions that protects them.

Firefly – A beetle that can glow in the dark and uses flashing patterns to communicate.

Hyaline layer – A thin layer in a scorpion's exoskeleton that glows under UV light.

Larvae – Baby insects, like wasps or flies, before they grow into adults.

Luna Moth – A large green moth that doesn't eat as an adult and lives about a week.

Midges – Tiny flying insects; only female biting midges bite humans.

Mucus – A slimy substance that worms produce to protect their skin and help them move.

Nocturnal – Animals that are awake at night.

Pheromones – Special chemicals animals use to communicate.

Proboscis – The long mouthpart of flies used to suck up liquid food.

Spinneret – The part of a spider that makes silk.

Solitary Wasps – Wasps that live alone, instead of in nests.

Swarm – The collective noun for wasps.

Venom – Poison that some animals, like scorpions or wasps, use to protect themselves or catch prey.

Can you remember what a group of wasps is called?
Turn back to page 21 to check if you were right!

About the Author

Stephanie was born on the Wirral and now lives in Nottingham with her husband, daughter, dogs, rabbits and hamster. She is an optician but when she is not testing eyes she can be found sewing, playing the harp, practising sign language, singing and/or adventuring with her family.

 Can you remember what a group of locusts is called?
Turn back to page 23 to check if you were right!

If you enjoyed A Click of Beetles, look out for our other collective noun books:

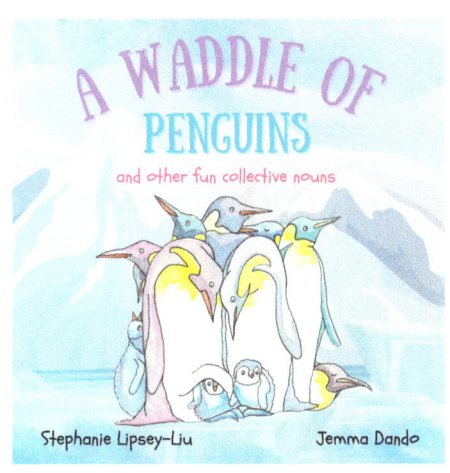
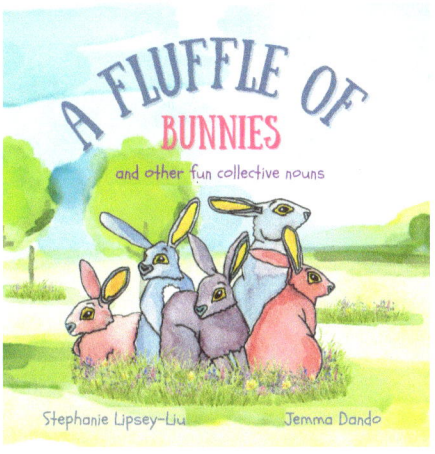
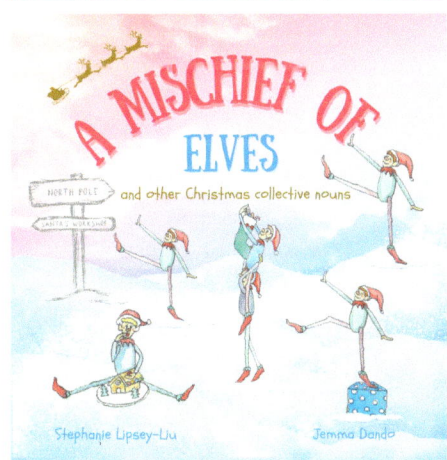
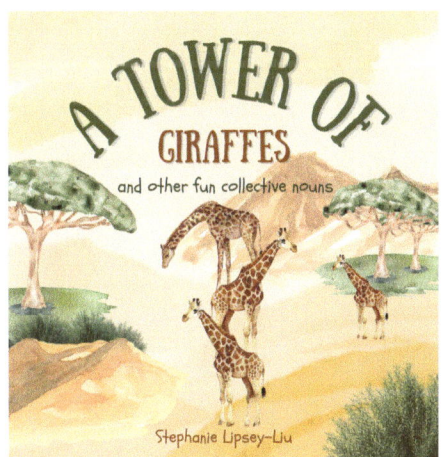

We would LOVE it if you could leave us a review on Amazon!

Ask your grown-up to help you write it.

If you'd like to share a picture of yourself reading any of our books, tag us on Facebook @littlelionpublishinguk or Instagram @littlelionpublishing.

www.ingramcontent.com/pod-product-compliance
Lightning Source LLC
Chambersburg PA
CBHW041120070526
44584CB00002B/223